DO NOT REMOVE
CARDS FROM POCKET

Diego Rivera

Diego Rivera, photographed in 1944.

JUNIOR ▪ WORLD ▪ BIOGRAPHIES

A JUNIOR *HISPANICS OF ACHIEVEMENT* BOOK

Diego
Rivera

DAVID SHIRLEY

CHELSEA JUNIORS

a division of CHELSEA HOUSE PUBLISHERS

English-language words that are italicized in the text can be found in the glossary at the back of the book.

Chelsea House Publishers

EDITORIAL DIRECTOR Richard Rennert
EXECUTIVE MANAGING EDITOR Karyn Gullen Browne
COPY CHIEF Robin James
PICTURE EDITOR Adrian G. Allen
CREATIVE DIRECTOR Robert Mitchell
ART DIRECTOR Joan Ferrigno
PRODUCTION MANAGER Sallye Scott

JUNIOR WORLD BIOGRAPHIES

SENIOR EDITOR Martin Schwabacher
SERIES DESIGN Marjorie Zaum

Staff for DIEGO RIVERA

EDITORIAL ASSISTANT Scott D. Briggs
PICTURE RESEARCHER Villette Harris
COVER ILLUSTRATION Patti Oleon

First Printing

1 3 5 7 9 8 6 4 2

Library of Congress Cataloging-in-Publication Data
Shirley, David
  Diego Rivera / David Shirley.
    p. cm.—(Junior world biographies)
  Includes bibliographical references and index.
ISBN 0-7910-2292-7
    1. Rivera, Diego, 1886–1957—Juvenile literature. 2. Artists—Mexico—Biography—Juvenile literature. [1. Rivera, Diego, 1886–1957. 2. Artists.]
I. Title. II. Series.
N6559.R58S55 1995
759.972—dc20   94-38696
[B]   CIP
                                                                    AC

Contents

Diego Rivera at work on his mural Man at the Crossroads *at Rockefeller Center in New York City.*

1

A Painter at the Crossroads

The great Mexican artist Diego Rivera could easily have stepped off the canvas of one of his own paintings. A huge bear of a man, Rivera stood six feet tall and weighed more than 300 pounds. When not chomping on a cigar, he had a wide, engaging smile and a quick wit that could charm just about anyone.

Wherever Rivera went, he was always the center of attention. Beautiful women lined up at parties to meet the rotund painter. Wealthy business leaders and heads of state invited him to their homes. Even Rivera's most bitter political enemies often forgot their differences when they met him in person.

Still, more than a few people were surprised when it was announced that the Rockefellers had hired Rivera to work for them. The wealthy New York family wanted him to paint a mural at their new business headquarters in midtown Manhattan. They planned to call the new complex Rockefeller Center. When completed, it was to feature 16 high-rise buildings. At the center of it all would be the RCA Building. Towering 70 stories above Sixth Avenue, it would become one of the world's great works of architecture. The Rockefellers wanted Rivera to paint a mural in the building's lobby.

To many, it seemed strange that Rivera would accept this project. Rivera was a committed communist. Communists believe that wealthy people like the Rockefellers should not be allowed to own huge amounts of money and property. They think that everything should be owned equally by ordinary working people. How could a communist like Rivera possibly paint a mural for one of the world's wealthiest families?

Rivera had first come to the United States in 1930 to paint a mural on the walls of the San Francisco Stock Exchange. There were plenty of protests at the time. Many people felt that a communist had no business working in the United States. The U.S. State Department agreed. For several months, Rivera was denied a work visa and his trip to the United States was delayed.

Things changed quickly, however, once Rivera began his work. In San Francisco, he painted a mural called *Allegory of California*. It was 30 feet tall. At the center of the painting was a beautiful woman with dark hair and bright eyes. Around her, Rivera painted the people of California at work. They included factory workers, farmers, shipbuilders, and engineers, and they all appeared happy and full of life.

Everyone who saw the painting was impressed—especially wealthy art patrons. Soon

Rivera received many offers to paint murals in the United States. Some of the same people who had at first wanted to keep Rivera out of the country now wanted to hire him to paint for them.

Nelson Rockefeller was one of the people who wanted to hire Rivera. He was the son of John D. Rockefeller and Abby Aldrich Rockefeller, one of the richest and most famous couples in the world. Only 24 years old when he first met Rivera, Rockefeller was already the director of the Museum of Modern Art and the executive vice president of Rockefeller Center. One day, he would become governor of California and then vice president of the United States.

Rockefeller hired Rivera to paint the lobby of his new building in 1933. He agreed to pay the artist $21,000 for his work. Even then, this was a small amount of money for such a large and time-consuming project. But Rivera was happy to do the painting. He knew that thousands of people would see his mural each day as they walked through the building on their way to work. Rivera believed that works of art should be placed in the midst of the people—not hidden away in galleries and museums.

The Rockefellers knew that Rivera was a communist. In Rivera's paintings, workers and poor people were always the heroes, while wealthy capitalists like the Rockefellers were usually portrayed as selfish and cruel. But the Rockefellers also knew that many people regarded Rivera as the greatest muralist in the world. They wanted to have the world's best painter cover the walls of their spectacular new building.

Before Rivera began, he showed Rockefeller a sketch of the mural he wanted to paint. He called it *Man at the Crossroads*. At its center was a man working at a huge machine. To the man's right, Rivera painted the world the way he wished it would be. Everyone looked happy and healthy, working side by side. There were no signs of poverty, hunger, or war. To the man's left, Rivera painted the world as it is. Wealthy capitalists ate, drank, and danced, while the poor huddled together in dark corners. To the side, a group of protesters were beaten by the police.

Several of the faces in Rivera's sketch were left blank. One of the blank faces belonged to a labor leader standing in the middle of a group of workers. For the completed painting, Rivera planned to use the face of Vladimir Lenin, the leader of the Soviet Revolution. Rivera did not tell Rockefeller about his plans. He later claimed that he did not think it was important. After all, the sketch that he showed Rockefeller had openly supported workers over capitalists. And Rivera had even made fun of the Rockefellers in one of his earlier paintings. He did not think they would be troubled by a picture of Lenin. He was wrong.

For several months, Rivera worked feverishly on the mural. At first, he only painted during the day. He would spend the evenings exploring New York City with his young wife, Frida Kahlo. Like Rivera, Kahlo was also a gifted painter. The two loved to walk the streets of New York together and visit the city's great museums.

Soon, however, Rivera did nothing but paint. He rarely stopped to eat, even when Kahlo brought food to the scaffold where he was working. Sometimes he would paint straight through the night.

Finally in April 1933, the mural was almost complete. One morning, Rivera climbed the scaffold and began to paint the face of Lenin. As usual, a large group of people had gathered to watch him work. The crowd grew restless as some people began to recognize the stern face of the great Soviet leader. Soon, more and more people were pouring into the building to view the portrait of Lenin for themselves.

News of the painting quickly spread throughout the country. Conservative newspapers and politicians condemned the Rockefellers for paying Rivera to glorify a communist leader. On April 2, 1933, the headline of New York's *World Telegram* announced angrily, "Rivera Perpetrates

Scenes of Communist Activity for RCA Walls—and Rockefeller Jr. Foots the Bill." Other angry headlines followed.

The Rockefellers were embarrassed by the controversy, and they were furious with Rivera. They had hoped that Rivera's mural would make their building an international landmark. Instead, it had made them look foolish. Less than two weeks after Rivera completed the painting, he received a letter from Nelson Rockefeller. The letter explained that the mural would have to be changed. Too many people had been offended by the picture of Lenin to allow it to remain in the painting. "I am afraid we must ask you to substitute the face of some unknown man," wrote Rockefeller.

Rivera refused. He offered to add the faces of Abraham Lincoln and other American heroes, but he would not remove the Soviet leader's face from the painting. Before replying to Rockefeller, however, Rivera asked one of his assistants to

Rivera caused a controversy by painting this picture of workers joining hands with the communist leader Lenin on the walls of the RCA Building at Rockefeller Center. The Rockefellers ordered Rivera to remove the portrait of Lenin, but he refused.

secretly photograph the mural. He knew that this might be the only record of his work.

Angered by Rivera's response, Rockefeller had the mural covered so that no one else could see it. Rivera was paid in full for his work and then dismissed. He was told that his painting would not remain in the lobby of the RCA Building.

People from all over the world protested Rockefeller's decision to cover the painting. Crowds gathered outside the building, demanding that the mural be shown to the public. Wealthy art patrons offered to buy the painting and move it to another site. Meanwhile, the Rockefellers promised not to harm the painting. But on February 10–11, 1934, they broke their promise. The entire mural was torn from the wall and destroyed.

By this time, Rivera was back home in Mexico City. The news broke his heart. He told a reporter that the Rockefellers had committed "an act of cultural vandalism." But Rivera did not grieve for long. He was soon back in New York

City, working on a mural for the New Workers School. He used the money he received from the Rockefellers to support himself while he completed the work. Later, he would paint a smaller version of *Man at the Crossroads* at the Palace of Fine Arts in Mexico City.

Rivera painted this portrait of a young boy in Mexico in 1927.

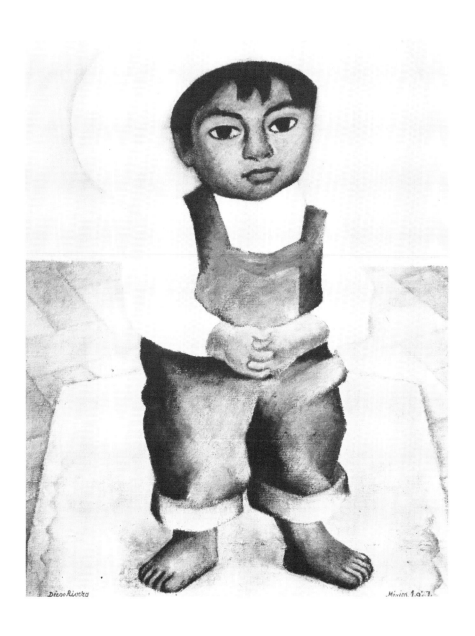

2

The Child
Artist

Even as a small child, Diego Rivera loved to draw. When he was only four years old, he was already covering the walls of his parents' home with pictures. At first, Diego's father and mother did everything they could to keep their pencils and pens out of the little boy's reach. But Diego was a clever child. He could always find something to use to mark up the walls and the furniture. Finally, Diego's father, who was also named Diego, gave in and rewarded his son with a brand new box of crayons. First, however, Diego senior covered the walls of the boy's room with paper. It was the future artist's first studio.

Diego's parents loved him very much, and they were always extremely patient with their son's strange ideas and unusual behavior. Before Diego was born, his mother had been pregnant four times, but the babies had all died at birth. When Diego's mother, María, was 26 years old and his father was 38, the couple decided to try one last time to have a child. María gave birth to a pair of healthy twins, Carlos and Diego, on December 8, 1886. It was no surprise that the Riveras decided to treat their only children with special care. Two years later, however, Carlos fell suddenly ill. Shortly after that, the child died, and Diego became the center of the family's attention.

Diego was raised in a tiny house in the middle of Guanajuato, an old mining town about 170 miles north of Mexico City. Guanajuato is perched along the edge of the Sierra Madre, a vast mountain range known for its beauty and its gold.

The people of the Sierra Madre are proud and brave. They were among the first groups of Mexicans to battle against Spain in the country's Wars of Independence. Growing up, Diego heard many stories of their great courage and the sacrifices that they had made for freedom. These stories would have a lasting impact on Diego. He would later include pictures of the early Mexican heroes in many of his paintings and murals.

After Diego's brother Carlos died, his mother became very depressed. For a long time, she remained near Carlos's grave, refusing to return home. When she started to feel better, she decided to become a doctor. To do this, she had to leave young Diego at home while she went away to school. During this time, Diego was cared for by an Indian nurse, a woman he grew to love even more than his mother. Throughout his life, Diego would always have a deep respect for the original Indian people of Mexico.

Diego also received the attention of his great-aunt Vicenta, whom the family called Totota. Unlike Diego's parents, Totota strongly disapproved of the boy's strong will and strange ideas. She felt that her unruly nephew needed more religious training, so she took young Diego to visit the local Catholic church and other religious shrines in the area. On one occasion, Totota urged Diego to pray that his mother would pass her exams. But Diego refused and his mother passed the tests anyway. After that, Diego had little use for religion.

Both of Diego's parents had grown up in poor homes without fathers. Diego's father was determined that his son would have a better life than he had had. He worked hard at several jobs to provide for his family. But Diego senior was also concerned about other children in Mexico. He wanted everyone to have plenty to eat and a good education.

During Diego's childhood, his father was an active member of the Liberal party, a political group that struggled to improve the lives of the poor. Diego Senior even started a weekly newspaper, *El Democrata.* The paper condemned the policies of the Mexican leader Porfirio Díaz. Díaz was part Indian and a former Mexican War hero. He had once bravely led the Mexican army against the French. Because of this, Diego's father had once supported Díaz, but he later came to feel that the former general had turned his back on the Mexican people.

Times were very hard in Guanajuato. There were few jobs, and many people had nothing to eat and no place to live. Unlike Diego's father, most people in town only cared about providing for their own families. Diego's father's radical political beliefs made many people angry.

In 1892, when Diego was six years old, an economic depression settled over Guanajuato. The silver mine that Diego's father was running at the time was forced to close. Diego senior was unable to find another job, and he moved the family to Mexico City. Jobs were said to be more plentiful in the huge Mexican capital. But times were tough even there. Diego's father had to take a low-paying job in the Department of Health.

After the move, Diego became very sick. He caught scarlet fever and then developed typhoid. Even after his health improved, Diego remained sad and inactive. He disliked Mexico City, and he missed his hometown. For an entire year, Diego stopped drawing.

Finally in 1894, when Diego was eight years old, he decided that he was ready to start school. His mother and his aunt Totota insisted that he be sent to a church school. Diego did well in school, even skipping a grade. But he had little interest in the religious lessons that he was required to study there.

Diego was very impressed, however, when Totota took him on a tour of local churches. He quickly fell in love with the beautiful religious artifacts—the carvings, statues, and paintings that lined the church walls. Mexican peasants and craftspeople had made all of these works of art by

Porfirio Díaz became a hero for leading the Mexican troops to victory against the French. After he became president in 1876, however, he turned the army against his political opponents in Mexico. When Diego Rivera demonstrated against Díaz at the age of 16, he was expelled from school.

hand. This was Diego's first exposure to the power and simplicity of Mexican folk art. For the rest of his life, Rivera would be an admirer of the peasant art he discovered that day.

When he was 10, Diego informed his parents that he had decided to become an artist. Of course, they disapproved. Good jobs were hard enough to find. No one was going to hire an artist in such difficult times. But Diego had made up his mind, and he soon began taking night classes at the Academy of San Carlos.

Diego finished high school with honors when he was only 12 years old. He promptly earned a scholarship to attend the Art Academy of the National Preparatory School. When he entered school the next year, he was much younger than most of the other students but unusually large for his age. Diego had always been a large child, but now, at 13, he was swelling into the wide, hefty figure of his later years. By the time he reached manhood, Diego would weigh more than 300 pounds.

At the academy, Diego saw classical European paintings for the first time. He also began to learn the classical approach to drawing, sculpting, and engraving. But he continued to be fascinated by Mexican folk art. He would often sneak away from classes to wander through the markets and churches of the villages just outside of Mexico City. He loved to watch the peasants and the poor Indian villagers go about their daily lives. It seemed to him that unlike people in the city, their lives were filled with color and imagination.

The biggest influence on Diego's art during this period was the great Mexican engraver and illustrator, Posada. Posada's eerie engravings and woodcuts filled the pages of Mexico City's radical newspapers and magazines. He created powerful images of poor people struggling against poverty and injustice. He made funny, insulting pictures of Mexico's rulers. He also made pictures of laughing skulls and dancing skeletons. Diego loved to watch Posada at work through the window of his tiny engraving shop. One day, Posada invited the young man inside to watch his work more closely. Diego would never forget the experience.

In 1903, Diego was expelled from school along with some other students for protesting against the Mexican government. The school eventually offered to let him return, but Diego had had enough of classrooms and rules. At 17, he stuffed his paints and brushes in a knapsack and began roaming the Mexican countryside.

Diego was still very young and immature, however. Without the discipline of school, he soon

This mural by Rivera, Feast of the Day of the Dead, *shows the influence of his one-time idol, Posada. Posada's mocking cartoons of political figures and eerie pictures of dancing skeletons impressed the young Rivera, who can be seen peeking out of his own painting at center-left, near the feet of the skeleton in overalls.*

began to eat and drink too much. For a while he quit painting to become a music hall performer. At one point, he feared that he was going blind. For the rest of his life, Diego would suffer from a host of imaginary illnesses.

Diego senior was worried about his son. He knew that the best thing for Diego would be a trip to Europe. There he could study the paintings of the European masters firsthand. Diego's father now had a better-paying job as a postal inspector, but he still did not have enough money to send his son abroad. One day, the older Rivera took a folder of his son's drawings to the governor of Veracruz, Teodoro Dehesa. The governor was so impressed with Diego's talent that he agreed to send the young man to Europe to study. He also arranged for Diego's living expenses. All Diego had to do was send the governor a new painting every six months.

Like most Mexican artists in Europe, Diego began his studies in Spain. At the Prado Museum in Madrid, he copied the great works of Brueghel,

Bosch, Goya, and El Greco. At night he roamed the streets of Madrid. A huge man, Diego walked around in wrinkled, paint-stained clothing. He now sported a thick, curly beard and a huge, broad-rimmed sombrero, or Mexican hat. Everywhere he went, people referred to him as the Mexican Cowboy. Even though he was fat and sloppy, people admired his talent as a painter and his playful intelligence.

Diego, however, was unhappy with his work at the time. "I did very little painting of any worth during the year and a half in Spain," he would later write. Diego's unhappiness with his work led him to eat and drink even more. From time to time, he would become disgusted with the weight he had gained, and he would try to starve himself. He was often very sick.

It was during this period that Diego first learned about Karl Marx. The author of *Capital* and *The Communist Manifesto,* Marx was the hero of many of the artists and writers who crowded the bars and cafés of Madrid. Marx's passionate writing about poverty and injustice would have a powerful influence on Diego's understanding of life and art. Rivera became an active member of the Communist party, and for the rest of his life politics and art would be his twin passions.

When Diego turned 22, he was tired of Spain and ready to start wandering again. With some other restless painters, he traveled throughout Europe, roaming across Portugal, France, Holland, England, and Belgium. In Belgium, Diego was reunited with María Gutierrez, a friend from his days in Madrid. Accompanying her was a young Russian artist named Angeline Beloff. She was attractive and fair, and Diego was immediately impressed. He would later describe her as, "a kind, sensitive, almost unbelievably decent person." Shortly after their meeting, Diego traveled with the two women to London.

A photograph of Rivera in 1944.

3

London, Paris, and Beyond

In London, Rivera and Beloff became inseparable. They walked together along lovely, tree-lined streets. They visited the city's great museums and saw some of the world's most beautiful buildings. But they also wandered sadly through the city's vast slums. There they saw many starving people and children begging for bread. They walked by rickety, wood-framed buildings, where several families lived crowded in a single apartment.

Karl Marx had studied poverty in London. The German philosopher wrote his great work *Capital* in the library at the University of London. As it had with Marx, seeing London fueled Rivera's outrage over the suffering of the poor and strengthened his commitment to radical politics and art.

One day, while visiting the British Museum, Rivera discovered a collection of Mexican art. The art works were made by Indians many years before his country was settled by the Spanish. The work had a powerful effect on the young painter. Years later, he would remember how he "suddenly felt an overmastering need to see my land and my people." He soon made arrangements with Governor Dehesa to return briefly to Mexico. The year was 1910, and Mexico was celebrating the 100th anniversary of its independence from Spain. In honor of the anniversary, Rivera was invited to display his most recent paintings at his old school, the Academy of San Carlos in Mexico City.

Leaving Europe was not an easy decision for Rivera. During his brief stay in London, he and Angeline Beloff had fallen in love. As he prepared to leave, the two vowed that they would live together in Paris when he returned from Mexico.

While Rivera was showing his work at San Carlos, the Mexican hillsides were exploding with rebellions against the Díaz government. All across the country, great Mexican rebels like Francisco "Pancho" Villa, Álvaro Obregón, and Emiliano Zapata were organizing armed revolts. Rivera did his part to support the rebels. He drew a poster to inspire the angry peasants. On the poster was a picture of a peasant family plowing a field. In the sky above them was a picture of Jesus. Below the picture, Rivera had written the message, "The Distribution of Land to the Poor Is Not Contrary to the Teachings of Our Lord Jesus Christ and the Holy Mother Church." Before he returned to Europe, Rivera also visited the city of Morelos, where he visited Zapata and his peasant troops.

Back in Paris in 1911, Rivera and Beloff moved into an apartment together in the lovely neighborhood of Montparnasse. It was an area filled with artists, intellectuals, and political rebels. Young people often stayed up all night in the neighborhood bars and cafés. There they would laugh and drink and argue over the ideas and events of the day.

Rivera's best friend during this period was a gifted, young Italian painter and sculptor named Amedeo Modigliani. He was one of the first 20th-century painters to study primitive art. His paintings of voluptuous nudes and blank-eyed children were among the most important artworks of the period. But Modigliani was a heavy drinker like Rivera, and he was also a drug addict. On most days and nights, the two men spent more time partying together in the local bars than they did painting.

In 1912, Rivera and Beloff traveled together to Spain. In the city of Toledo, Rivera spent several months studying the work of the great Spanish painter El Greco. In Spain, Rivera was also introduced to the new style of painting called cubism. First practiced by Georges Braque and Pablo Picasso, cubism broke down everything in nature into flat shapes and forms. In a cubist painting, a face might look like a triangle, a foot like a box, and a belly like a big circle. Most people and things in cubist paintings were very hard to recognize.

This painting, Sailor, *is one of more than 200 Rivera painted in the style known as cubism, which portrays objects from many angles at once using basic shapes such as squares and circles. Rivera's experiments with cubism won him great praise, but he eventually decided to seek a form of art "truer to my inmost feelings."*

During the next few years, Rivera produced more than 200 cubist paintings. He even became known as one of the most important cubist painters. But he was never truly happy with the style. He felt that it was too difficult for most people to enjoy. And he believed that it had little to do with the things that were important in life. "I would surrender all the glory and acclaim that cubism had brought me for a way in art truer to my inmost feelings," he wrote years later.

These were difficult years throughout the world. In Mexico, the revolution against Díaz was already in full swing. In 1913, President Francisco Madero was assassinated, and Rivera's funding was temporarily cut off. The following year an even more important event occurred when Archduke Francis Ferdinand of Austria was assassinated. This marked the beginning of World War I. The great war would continue for four years. It was one of the bloodiest conflicts ever fought. Everywhere that Rivera traveled, he met people whose lives had been disrupted by the war.

The war also put an end to Rivera's late-night partying. In Paris, the bars and cafés now closed early each night. There was one happy event during this period, however. On August 11, 1916, Beloff gave birth to a son whom they named Diego.

In the spring of 1917, the United States joined the war, after half the French army refused to continue fighting. On the other side of Europe, the Russian soldiers also left the front. Led by Leon Trotsky and Vladimir Lenin, Russian troops joined factory workers in the cities to start a revolution against the czar. Inspired by the writings of Karl Marx, Lenin and Trotsky would create a communist government in Russia.

Rivera was captivated by the news of the communist revolt in Russia. Finally, poor people and working people were taking control of their own lives and building their own society. This made Rivera hopeful that the People's Revolution in Mexico might also be successful.

The talk of revolution made Rivera even

more frustrated with cubism. More than ever, he longed to paint in a way that would capture the imaginations of ordinary men and women. Rivera began to study the work of the Dutch masters of the 17th century and the French portrait painter Pierre-Auguste Renoir. These paintings portrayed the everyday lives of common people. They were full of color and humor and a genuine passion for life.

Conditions were so bad in Paris that Rivera and Beloff sent their son to live with friends in the suburbs shortly after he was born. When the boy was two years old, he came home to live with his parents. But Rivera and Beloff were still very poor. They had little food to give their child, and the apartment was extremely cold in the winter. Before the winter ended, the young child became ill and died.

In 1919, Rivera met a young Mexican artist living in Paris named David Alfaro Siqueiros. The young painter had just arrived from Mexico, where he had fought in the revolution. Rivera was eager to hear stories of the triumphs and sacrifices of the Mexican peasants. Rivera was saddened to hear that the great peasant leader Zapata had been murdered on April 10, 1919. Zapata was one of the true heros of the Mexican Revolution, and his death was a great blow to the peasant army.

Rivera enjoyed listening to Siqueiros's ideas about painting. Like Rivera, the young artist believed that art should be used to inspire the poor and support the revolution. The two men sometimes stayed up all night talking about painting and the Mexican Revolution. Two years later, Siqueiros would publish a book, *Calls to the Plastic Artists in America,* based on his conversations with Rivera.

In 1920, Rivera decided that it was time to do something with his new ideas. He had just received a large sum of money for painting a portrait of a French ambassador and his wife. He used the money to travel to Italy, where he spent 17 months studying the frescoes of the great Italian painters. Frescoes are paintings made on wet plaster. Rivera was particularly impressed by the paintings of Michelangelo. Rivera spent several weeks examining the 16th-century painter's famous fresco on the ceiling of the Sistine Chapel in Rome. Rivera admired how Michelangelo had used only nine panels to tell the entire biblical story of Genesis.

In 1920, the revolutionary leader Obregón was elected president of Mexico. With Obregón in charge, Rivera was finally ready to return home. In June of the following year, Rivera sailed for

A portrait of Angeline Beloff drawn by Rivera in 1917. Rivera lived with Beloff for several years in Europe, and the two had a son, Diego, who died at the age of two. Rivera eventually abandoned Beloff and returned to Mexico.

Mexico. He left Beloff behind in Paris, but he promised to send for her as soon as he had enough money.

Rivera had spent 14 years away from his native country. "On my arrival in Mexico," he later wrote, "I was struck by the inexpressible beauty of that rich and severe, wretched and exuberant land."

Rivera had little time to relax. Shortly after his arrival, he was sent on a tour of the country by the minister of education, José Vasconcelos. The artist visited the southern Yucatán Peninsula, where peasant revolutionaries were setting up their own government. Everywhere he went, he saw bright, red communist flags. At the Mayan ruins of Chichén Itzá, he visited the Temple of the Tigers. There he saw enormous frescoes that had been painted 400 years before Michelangelo.

Rivera was overwhelmed by the great works of native Mexicans. He realized that the inspiration he had sought in Europe had been waiting for him in Mexico all along. Rivera became determined to create a genuine Mexican style. He wanted Mexican painting to be free from classical European influences. He felt it should draw instead on the great wealth of Mexican folk tradition.

Minister Vasconcelos was happy to give Rivera the chance to try out his new ideas about painting. He commissioned the artist to paint a series of murals on the walls of public buildings throughout Mexico City. Rivera's first mural was at the National Preparatory School, where he had studied painting as a child. His second mural was in the building that housed the Ministry of Public Education.

Vasconcelos was thrilled with the murals. But Rivera was still unhappy with his work. The paintings were peopled with Mexican workers and peasants, but Rivera's style was too European. He knew that he would have to work very hard to create a truly Mexican style. For the next several years, he worked day and night on his art. He painted hundreds of frescoes throughout the country. He also made woodcuts, mosaics, stained-glass windows, and drawings for magazines. He even did stage designs for plays written and performed by Mexican workers.

Rivera broke his promise to Angeline Beloff and never sent for her. She continued to wait for him in Paris. But in 1922, he married a beautiful woman named Lupe Marin. Rivera and Beloff would never speak again. In 1933, she traveled briefly to Mexico and actually approached her former lover in a concert hall, but Rivera acted as if he did not recognize her and turned away.

Rivera did not really forget Beloff, however. "She gave me everything a good woman can give to a man," he would later confess. "In return, she received from me all the heartache and misery that a man can inflict upon a woman."

Beloff saw things differently. "Given my life to live over again," she said toward the end of her life, "I would still choose to live those ten years over again with him."

According to Rivera, meeting his second wife, Frida Kahlo, was "the most important fact in my life."

4

The Great
Muralist

During the 1920s, Mexico City became one of the art capitals of the world, and Rivera was the city's most famous artist. People traveled great distances to see the wonderful murals that filled the walls of buildings and public squares throughout the city. Young artists came from many different countries to study with Rivera. Eventually, a whole group of local painters also became gifted muralists under Rivera's influence. Among the best of them were Fernando Leal, Jean Charlot, Amado de la Cueva, and Rivera's old friend David Siqueiros.

After Rivera, Mexico's most famous and gifted painter was the great muralist José Orozco. The Mexican people called him El Tigre, or the Tiger. Orozco was Rivera's chief rival, and, for a while, the two men despised each other. Orozco once said that Rivera's paintings were a "poor imitation" of Indian folk art. Rivera accused Orozco of being overly sensitive to criticism and producing vulgar paintings. But the two men soon came to respect one another. Rivera was particularly impressed by Orozco's mural, *Revolutionary Trinity*. "Good painting and deep emotion, such beautiful work," he said when he saw it.

Rivera and Siqueiros led efforts to form a trade union for artists in Mexico City. They called it the Union of Technical Workers, Painters and Sculptors. At the height of his fame, Rivera received only two dollars a day for his work for the government. He was proud that he was paid and treated as an ordinary worker. He hoped that other painters would join together to show their support for each other and for other workers throughout the country.

Many people, however, disliked the idea of a union for artists. They felt that each artist should be independent and that everyone should be free to pursue his or her own vision. Some people were so angry with Rivera that they tried to destroy several of his murals. Some of his paintings were badly damaged. Student gangs even resorted to violence. A group of Rivera's followers were attacked on the street. During this period, Rivera always kept a gun at his side while painting.

But Rivera was too busy to worry about the controversy. He was always working on several projects at once. He worked so much that his huge, colorful murals were gradually beginning to fill the city's walls. His major achievement was the great series of murals that decorated the Ministry of Education building. Almost every inch of the three-story, two-block building was covered with scenes from Rivera's brush. In all, Rivera com-

This mural from Rivera's History of Mexico *cycle entitled* Cortez in Mexico *depicts the Spanish conquistadors, who enslaved the Mexican peasants, as grotesque and deformed ogres.*

pleted 124 frescoes for the building—more than 17,000 square feet of painting! The project took him more than five years to complete.

In August 1924, Lupe Marin gave birth to a daughter name Lupe. The couple nicknamed the baby Pico, which means "pointy head." But Rivera was so busy with his work that he neglected his wife and his newborn child. He also ignored his health and his appearance. Sometimes he would work for several days without returning home to change his clothes or take a bath. When he finally did wander home, Lupe would tell him that he smelled bad and refuse to go near him.

In 1926, Rivera began painting the chapel of the Chapingo School. This was his first chance to use what he had learned from the frescoes of Michelangelo in the Sistine Chapel in Rome. Rivera painted every inch of wall space in the chapel. He colored the windows with bright, beautiful pictures of Mexican peasants. And like Michelangelo, he even covered the chapel's ceiling with one of his frescoes.

Rivera fell from a scaffold while he was painting the chapel's ceiling. Workers found him unconscious and bleeding on the floor. When he awoke, he discovered that he was badly injured. Rivera spent three months at home in bed. While he was recovering, Lupe gave birth to a second daughter, whom they named Ruth. For a while, Rivera spent time with his family, but as soon as he was well, he returned to the same punishing work schedule as before.

Somehow Rivera still managed to find time for politics. In 1926, he joined the Hands-Off Nicaragua Committee, a radical group that sought to force U.S. troops out of the tiny Central American country. In 1927, Rivera arranged to travel to the Soviet Union for the 10th anniversary of the Soviet Revolution. It was his first trip to the powerful communist nation. Before he left, Rivera gave his wife permission to court other men. "I welcomed the invitation to the Soviet Union as [an excuse] to get away from her," he would later tell a friend. Shortly after Rivera sailed for the Soviet

Union, Marin divorced him and married the poet Jorge Cuesta.

Rivera spent six months in the Soviet Union. He loved the country's vast landscapes, its great architecture, and the hard work and enthusiasm of the Soviet people. But he hated Soviet painting. He found it stuffy and conservative. Rivera's meeting with Soviet leader Joseph Stalin was a complete disaster. The two strong-willed men disagreed about everything, and Rivera finally stomped angrily out of the room. Soon after, Rivera was asked to leave the country. He was happy to go.

When he returned to Mexico, Rivera became even more involved in politics. In 1928, he managed the presidential campaign of Communist party candidate Pedro Rodríguez Triana. He also helped defend his friend Tina Modotti, who was falsely accused of murdering her lover. In spite of Rivera's efforts, Modotti was convicted of the crime and forced to leave the country. But Rivera and his friends would not give up on the case. Eventually, they found information proving she was innocent, and she was allowed to return home.

In 1929, Rivera was appointed director of the Academy of San Carlos. At the Academy, he was able to put his radical ideas about painting to work. He refused to let students copy the works of European masters, which was the usual method for teaching young artists. He wanted them to discover their own unique styles. And to give them an understanding of the lives of workers, who are the backbone of society in communist belief, Rivera insisted that all students spend their days working in a factory.

Around that time, Rivera met a brilliant young artist named Frida Kahlo. Several years earlier, Kahlo had been a student at the National Preparatory School, where she was part of a student gang called the Cachuchas. The Cachuchas loved to play practical jokes. Sometimes they would throw water balloons or firecrackers at other painters while they worked. Kahlo especially loved to pick on Rivera. With his huge body and his scandalous personal life, he was an easy target for insults. Rivera enjoyed the young woman's teasing, but when he met her years later he did not remember her, although she remembered him.

Frida Kahlo had overcome many hardships before she met Rivera. When she was six, she developed polio. The disease permanently damaged her legs, and she always wore long dresses to keep people from seeing her condition. In 1925, when she was 18, she was in a terrible accident. A trolley car collided with the bus that she was riding. Several of her bones were fractured, and her hip and back were badly broken. For the rest of her life, she would suffer from terrible pain due to the injuries.

Like Rivera, Kahlo was as proud and rebellious as she was gifted. She had many lovers, including a long affair with the handsome leader of the Cachuchas, Alejandro Gómez. She also angered many people by having affairs with other women.

Kahlo and Rivera fell deeply in love. Kahlo's friends could not understand how she could possibly be attracted to Rivera, who was very fat and more than 20 years her senior. But Kahlo was as captivated by Rivera as he was with her. He was immediately charmed by her wit and her intelligence. He would later confide that meeting Kahlo was "the most important fact in my life." She called him her "Frog Prince," because of his large body and bulging eyes. In spite of the public's disapproval, the two were married in 1929.

Soon after, Rivera was expelled from the Communist party. The party's leaders insisted that Rivera had betrayed the Mexican people by continuing to paint murals for the conservative government, even though his paintings attacked the country's rulers. Kahlo immediately quit the party to show her support for her husband. The 43-year-old painter behaved proudly throughout the controversy, but the party's decision hurt him very badly.

Things got even worse the following year when he was fired from his position as director of the Academy of San Carlos because of his radical politics. But times were hard for all of Rivera's friends. Siqueiros had been thrown in jail earlier in the year for his political activities. Orozco had been forced to leave the country in 1927 and was now teaching and painting in the United States.

Art patrons had been trying to lure Rivera to the United States for many years. By 1930, he feared that Mexico was not safe for someone with his political views, and he accepted an invitation to paint a mural at the San Francisco Stock Exchange. Artists and art collectors in the United States were thrilled to hear that Rivera was finally coming. But the U.S. State Department did not share their excitement. As a former member of the Communist party, Rivera was viewed as an enemy of the U.S. government. (Years earlier, Soviet leader Lenin had vowed to one day overthrow the U.S. political system.) For several months, Rivera's

Rivera puts the finishing touches on his fresco for the walls of the San Francisco Stock Exchange, his first mural in the United States. Entitled Allegory of California, *it honors the working people of the state.*

request for a work visa was denied. Finally, in November 1930, Rivera and Kahlo arrived in San Francisco.

Exploring San Francisco with Kahlo in 1930 reminded Rivera of his experience in London with Angeline Beloff 20 years earlier. The couple was fascinated by the city's trolley cars and rolling hills. They admired the beautiful mansions of the Russian Hill neighborhood. But they were also deeply saddened by the poverty they saw everywhere. The long lines of unemployed people waiting for bread and soup horrified them.

After Rivera completed the San Francisco mural, he received many more offers to paint in the United States. He was hired by Edsel Ford, the son of Henry Ford, to paint a mural at the Detroit Institute of Arts. Rivera spent two months making sketches of the Ford Motor Company's plant in Dearborn, Michigan. Even as a child, Rivera had loved to draw machines. He was thrilled to paint a mural celebrating the relationship between men and machines. Rivera would later refer to this

27-panel fresco, called *Detroit Industry*, as "the great saga of machine and steel." Many people consider it to be his finest painting in the United States.

In spite of their political beliefs, Rivera and Kahlo lived like rich people while they were in the United States. They even became close friends with some of their wealthy patrons. But they also faced difficult challenges during this period. Fearful for his health, Rivera went on a punishing diet and lost more than 100 pounds. Kahlo desperately wanted to have a child, but she had been unable to give birth since her accident. She twice tried to have a baby with Rivera, but both pregnancies ended in miscarriage. After the second attempt, Kahlo became deeply depressed. Rivera could not understand her sadness. He felt that art was much more important than having a child. "For me painting and life are one," he often said.

Kahlo realized that Rivera's passion for his painting would always be greater than his love for her. "I cannot speak of Diego as my husband, because that term when applied to him is an absurdity," she once wrote. "He has never been, nor will he ever be, anybody's husband."

After Detroit, Rivera went to New York City to paint the RCA murals. When they were destroyed by the Rockefellers, Rivera began painting at the New Workers School in New York. The school was run by the followers of Leon Trotsky. The radical Soviet leader had recently been banished from his country for criticizing Joseph Stalin. Around the world, many people were accepting Trotsky's ideas. They said that he, not Stalin, was now the true voice of the Worker's Revolution. Rivera had always despised Stalin, and he quickly declared his support for Trotsky.

Diego Rivera and his wife, Frida Kahlo, demonstrate against fascism in Mexico City. Both were devoted members of the Communist party who supported workers and peasants in their struggles against the rich.

5
The Final Years

Rivera became very depressed after he returned to Mexico in 1935. He was still upset about the destruction of the RCA murals. And without a new project to occupy him, he spent much of his time brooding. Kahlo wrote to a friend, "Because he does not feel well he has not begun painting... he thinks that everything that is happening to him is my fault, because I made him come to Mexico."

In reality, however, it was Rivera who had made Kahlo unhappy. His numerous affairs with other women had deeply hurt his wife. While in New York, he had a brief relationship with the artist Louise Nevelson. And back in Mexico, he soon became involved with Kahlo's sister Christina. Angry and humiliated, Frida moved into her own apartment and later left for New York City. But she refused to divorce her husband. "At bottom, you and I love each other dearly," she wrote to Rivera from New York. "We will always love each other."

Finally Rivera grew tired of Christina. Frida soon forgave both Rivera and her sister and returned to the house she shared with Rivera in San Angel. The couple continued to live in separate quarters, however. Now it was Kahlo's turn to have affairs, with both men and women. Rivera had never been faithful in any of his relationships with women, but it always caused him pain to hear of Kahlo's affairs.

Rivera was also hurt by the end of his friendship with Siqueiros. After Rivera was expelled from the Communist party, the two men became bitter political enemies. On August 26, 1935, at a conference on education, their hatred of each other almost resulted in violence. In the middle of a heated debate on art and revolution, the two former friends both drew pistols and ended the conference by pointing guns in each other's faces.

In 1936, Leon Trotsky was living in Norway. He had escaped to Scandinavia from his native Russia. A Soviet tribunal had sentenced him to death for treason against the Stalin government. Under pressure from their Soviet neighbors, the Norwegian government finally told Trotsky that he would have to leave the country. He desperately needed a safe place to live. Rivera invited Trotsky to come and stay with him in Mexico.

On January 9, 1937, Trotsky and his wife Natalia arrived in Mexico. For the next two years, the couple lived at Kahlo's house in Coyoacán. Shortly after his arrival, Trotsky and Kahlo had a brief affair. But his closest followers advised him to break off the relationship. Trotsky could not afford a public scandal if he wanted to challenge Stalin's rule in the Soviet Union. Trotsky ended his affair with Kahlo and returned to his wife. A few months later, Kahlo presented Trotsky with a self-portrait for his birthday.

Over the years, Kahlo had continued to paint, though often in her famous husband's shadow. By the late 1930s, however, her strange, sensual self-portraits were beginning to attract attention in galleries around the world.

While Kahlo was in Paris for an exhibition of her work, Rivera entertained the Trotskys. The two men argued constantly. Although both Rivera and Trotsky enjoyed the debates at first, their arguments grew more serious after the outbreak of war in Europe. Finally, Rivera resigned from Trotsky's political party, the Fourth International, and the former Soviet leader and his wife moved out of Kahlo's apartment.

When Kahlo returned from Paris, she and Rivera decided to end their marriage. Neither of them ever spoke publicly about the reason for their separation. Some suspected that Rivera's affair with Paulette Goddard might have been the cause.

Goddard was a beautiful actress who had starred in many of Charlie Chaplin's greatest films. She lived across the street from Rivera, and the two were often seen together.

After Trotsky broke with Rivera, several attempts were made on the former Soviet leader's life. For a while, many people suspected that Rivera was involved. But Rivera made clear to everyone that he hated Stalin even more than Trotsky. On one occasion, Rivera's former friend Siqueiros tried to kill Trotsky. Arriving on horseback, he and a group of armed men fired guns repeatedly into the Trotskys' home. The couple hid safely under the bed, however. Siqueiros was arrested and exiled to Chile.

On August 20, 1940, Trotsky was murdered by one of his followers, Jacques Mornard. Kahlo and Mornard had been friends, and she was briefly considered a suspect in the murder.

Rivera was in San Francisco at the time of Trotsky's death, working on a new mural. Alone in Mexico, Kahlo's health began to fail. When he learned that she was sick, Rivera invited her to come live with him. On December 8, 1940, the two were married for the second time. "I'm going to marry her because she really needs me," Rivera confided to his friends before the ceremony.

Germany invaded the Soviet Union in June of 1941. With Hitler and the Nazis now threatening the world, Rivera decided to make his peace with Stalin and the Communist party. As bad as Stalin was, Rivera reasoned, Hitler was much worse. But the Soviets were no longer interested in Rivera. For the next 14 years, he would repeatedly be denied membership in the Communist party.

By 1943, the Mexican government and the Communist party were united in the fight against Nazi Germany. The government was happy to have Rivera back as an ally. Both he and Kahlo were offered positions as teachers at the National School of Painting and Sculpture. Kahlo eventually became too sick to travel to the school. But several of her students moved to Coyoacán to continue their studies with her. The couple also worked together on a plan to build an art museum near Coyoacán. The museum was dedicated to the country's rich tradition of Indian art. Eventually, it would hold more than 60,000 works of art.

In 1944, Rivera and Kahlo separated for the second time. Two years later, she traveled to New York for back surgery. But her condition became even worse following the operation. The doctors could offer Kahlo little hope that she would ever get better. Faced with this news, she became increasingly depressed. In many of her self-portraits from this period, she depicted herself as sad and tearful. Kahlo spent the remainder of her life in and out of the hospital. She endured several painful operations to fight the infection that was slowly destroying her bones. Nothing worked, but Rivera was constantly at her side. In April 1953, the doctors informed the couple that Kahlo's right leg would have to be amputated. "This is going to kill her," Rivera said to a friend.

For the rest of her life, Kahlo was confined to a wheelchair. On July 2, 1954, she made her final public appearance. She joined Rivera and 10,000 other marchers to protest the U.S.–backed invasion of Guatemala. Kahlo raised her fist defiantly from her wheelchair and shouted, "Gringos asesinos, fuera!" (Yankee assassins, get out!) Kahlo developed pneumonia shortly after the march. On July 13, 1954, she died quietly in her sleep. Rivera was painting in his studio at the time.

Before the funeral, Kahlo's coffin was left open at the Palace of Fine Arts in Mexico City. Thousands of people came to pay their respects. Rivera angered many people by draping a huge red Communist flag across the coffin. He later called it "the most tragic day of my life." In 1957, Rivera opened Kahlo's house in Coyoacán to the public as the Frida Kahlo Museum.

While Kahlo's health had been failing, Rivera's career had been reaching new heights. In August 1949, a 50-year retrospective of his paintings was held at the Palace of Fine Arts in Mexico City. He was 64 years old. Three years later, the National Institute of Fine Arts commissioned him to paint a mural that would be seen throughout Europe in a special exhibition of Mexican art. And on September 14, 1954—just two months after Kahlo's death—the Mexican Communist party finally readmitted Rivera.

The following year, Rivera married Emma Hurtado, a gallery owner and art dealer, shortly before leaving on his second tour of the Soviet Union. Rivera became sick in the Soviet Union and had to be hospitalized. Some doctors suspected that he was suffering from cancer. "I love Moscow and I love the Soviet Union," he told a reporter at the time. "If I have to die of cancer, I should die here." But Rivera returned to Mexico at the end of the year, just in time for his 70th birthday. The Mexican government had declared it a day of national celebration.

Rivera's health never fully recovered after his illness in the Soviet Union. He tried to stay cheerful and keep painting. He was now one of the most famous artists in the world and a national treasure in his native Mexico. He had spent his entire life working for these honors. Unfortunately, he would have little time to enjoy them. In September 1957, a blood clot caused him to lose the use of his right arm. He would never paint again. Two months later, shortly after midnight on November 24, 1957, Rivera died of heart failure. It was just two weeks before his 71st birthday.

Like Kahlo, Rivera's body was displayed for the public at the Palace of Fine Arts. The Mexican government honored him as a fallen hero. Thousands of mourners filed through the hall to catch one last glimpse of their country's greatest artist. At the funeral, a group of communists unfurled the red flag of the Communist party. As a final tribute,

Rivera makes a quick sketch in Moscow, the capital of the former Soviet Union. Rivera told an interviewer, "I love Moscow and I love the Soviet Union. If I have to die of cancer I should die here."

Rivera was buried at the city's Rotunda of Illustrious Men at the Pantheon of Dolores.

In the years following Rivera's death, his work has become increasingly popular. His paintings hang in the world's finest museums, alongside the European masters whose work he once studied. People travel from around the world to view his great murals in Mexico City.

All of this would have pleased Rivera. He loved fame and craved recognition for his work. What would have pleased him even more, however, is how his work has influenced a new generation of artists. In recent years, socially committed artists like Keith Haring and Sue Coe have brought renewed attention to murals and frescoes. And in cities around the world, anonymous urban muralists use city walls to tell their stories and record the history of their communities. More than all the gallery paintings and museum pieces, perhaps this would have pleased Rivera most of all.

Further Reading

Cockcroft, James. *Diego Rivera*. New York: Chelsea House, 1991.

Diego Rivera. Milwaukee: Raintree, 1988.

Garza, Hedda. *Frida Kahlo*. New York: Chelsea House, 1994.

Karl Marx. New York: Franklin Watts, 1987.

Killingray, David. *The Mexican Revolution*. Saint Paul: Greenhaven, 1980.

O'Brien, Steven. *Pancho Villa*. New York: Chelsea House, 1994.

Glossary

assassinate   to murder a political leader

capitalist   a wealthy person, such as a factory owner, who hires others to work for him

commission   to hire someone to create a work of art

communist   one who believes the economic system of capitalism is unfair because a small group of people own most of society's wealth

controversy   a big fuss or disagreement

mosaic   a picture made from a pattern of small tiles

mural   a huge painting made directly on a wall

retrospective   a major exhibit showing work from an artist's entire career

scaffold   a temporary framework with platforms allowing people to work above the ground

woodcut   a print made from a piece of wood with a design carved into it

Chronology

Dec. 8, 1886	Diego Rivera is born in Guanajuato, Mexico
1907	Goes to Europe with the support of the governor of Veracruz
1909	Falls in love with Russian artist Angeline Beloff
1910	Mexican Revolution begins
1912	Rivera begins experimentation with cubism
1919	Meets Mexican artist David Alfaro Siqueiros
1920	Goes to Italy to study Renaissance art; Obregón elected president of Mexico
1921	Rivera returns to Mexico, where he becomes fascinated with ancient Mexican art; decides to create a genuine Mexican style

1922	Commissioned to paint series of murals in Mexico City; marries Lupe Marin
1927	Visits Soviet Union; divorces Marin
1929	Appointed director of the Academy of San Carlos; marries Frida Kahlo; expelled from Communist party
1930	Fired from the Academy of San Carlos; goes to California to paint San Francisco Stock Exchange mural
1933–34	Causes controversy with the RCA Building murals, which are eventually destroyed by the Rockefellers
1949	Fifty-year retrospective held at the Palace of Fine Arts in Mexico City
1954	Kahlo dies
1955	Rivera marries Emma Hurtado; visits Soviet Union
Nov. 24, 1957	Dies of heart failure

Index

David Shirley has written several books for children including biographies of Gloria Estefan, Alex Haley, Satchel Paige, and Malcolm X. He is a contributing editor to *Option* magazine, and his rock music criticism has also appeared in *Rolling Stone* and *Spin*. Shirley grew up in Tupelo, Mississippi, Elvis's birthplace, and currently lives in Brooklyn, New York, where his hobby is watching bats in Prospect Park.

Picture Credits